Good Curling

From the Wiggle River Curling Club of Wiggle River MN.

Written and Illustrated by Franklin Haws Jr.

This book is dedicated to my
family, Ann and Seth.
Thank you for your patience.

And to my Plan B
curling teammates,
especially Terri and Mike.

KIM AND KIMMY FALKENBERG ARE BELIEVED TO BE THE FIRST CURLERS TO SET FOOT IN MINNESOTA IN 1879...

...BUT SADLY, THEY BROUGHT NOTHING BUT CURLING GEAR AND THEIR NAMES DISAPPEARED FROM THE CENSUS ROLES IN 1880.

AT LEAST CURLING SURVIVED THAT WINTER AND THRIVES TO THIS DAY.

IN 2018, THE U.S. CURLING TEAM WON GOLD MEDALS AT THE PYEONGCHANG WINTER OLYMPICS. THAT NIGHT, EVERYTHING WENT RIGHT FOR THE TEAM FROM THE UPPER MIDWEST.

WELL...ALMOST.

WHAT THE HECK?

WAIT A SECOND...

GUYS, THEY GAVE US THE WOMEN'S CURLING GOLD MEDAL...

(THEY WERE GIVEN THE CORRECT GOLD MEDALS WITHIN MINUTES, BUT STILL...)

OVERNIGHT, THE FIVE OLYMPIC CURLING TEAM MEMBERS BECAME NATIONAL HEROES AND INTEREST IN THE SPORT OF CURLING EXPLODED ACROSS THE COUNTRY.

TAKING ADVANTAGE OF THAT INTEREST, CURLING CLUBS OPENED IN CITIES AND TOWNS ACROSS THE U.S. BY PEOPLE LOOKING TO BE PART OF WHAT WAS CALLED THE *HURRY HARD TIDAL WAVE*. LIKE THE RAILROAD BARRONS OF THE 1800s, FORTUNES WERE MADE OVERNIGHT.

SO IN 2019, IN THE SMALL MINNESOTA LOGGING TOWN OF WIGGLE RIVER, ONE COUPLE INVESTED THEIR LIFE SAVINGS AND OPENED THE WIGGLE RIVER CURLING CLUB.

THE CURLING CLUB MADE SCOTTY FITZ AND WIFE FELDA MILLIONAIRES OVERNIGHT. THEY RESHAPED THEIR LIVES INTO WHAT THEY CONSIDERED THE MOST GLAMOROUS TIME IN U.S. HISTORY, THE 1920s.

WITH APOLOGIES TO JOHN HELD JR

WIGGLE RIVER CURLING CLUB

MEET A FEW MEMBERS AND EMPLOYEES THE WIGGLE RIVER CURLING CLUB.

Daisy Allison
Skip-Curling Skulls
Dairy farmer

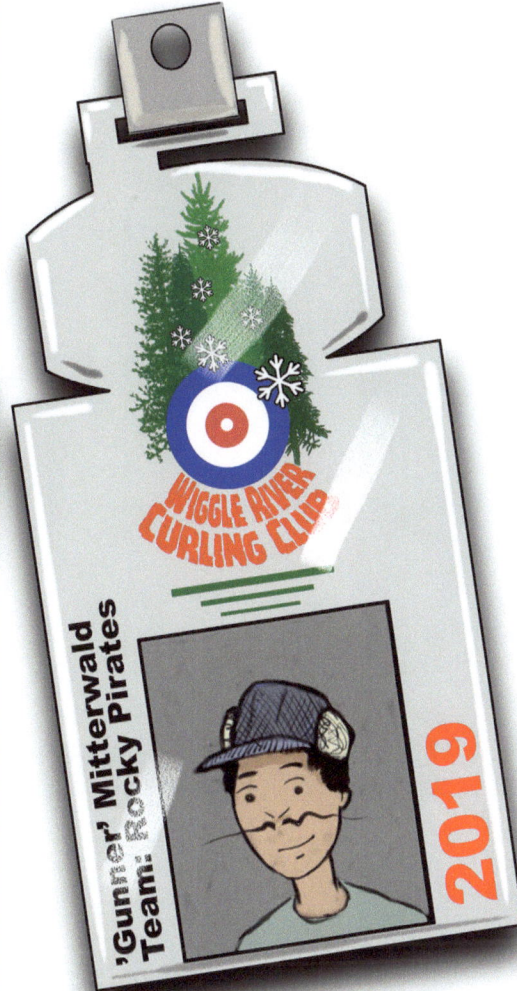

Steve "Gunner" Mitterwald
3rd / 2nd-Curling Skulls
LCDR Coast Guard (Ret)

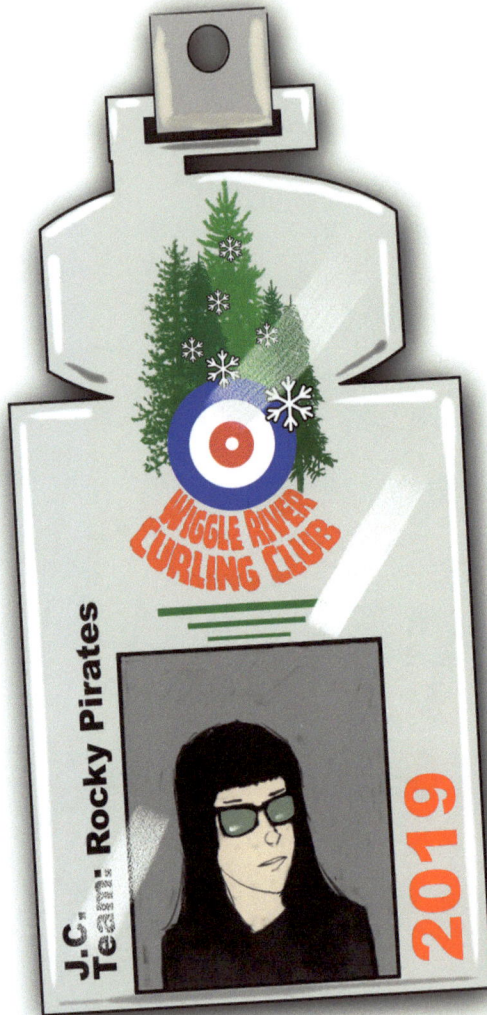

J.C.
1st-Curling Skulls
Singer/Songwriter

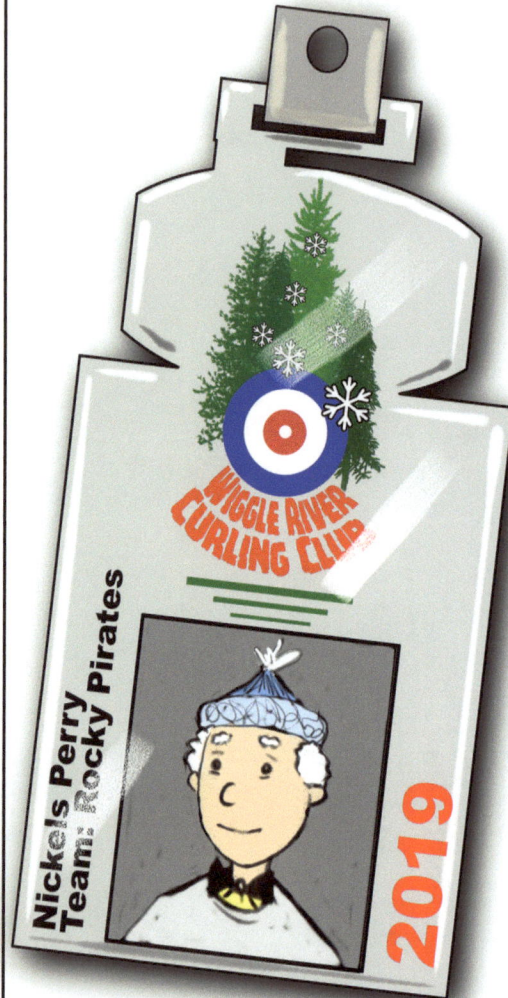

Nickels Perry
3rd / 2nd-Curling Skulls
Banker

**Julius Henry
Ice Master**

Dr.
**Club Research and
Development Manager**

14

15

16

18

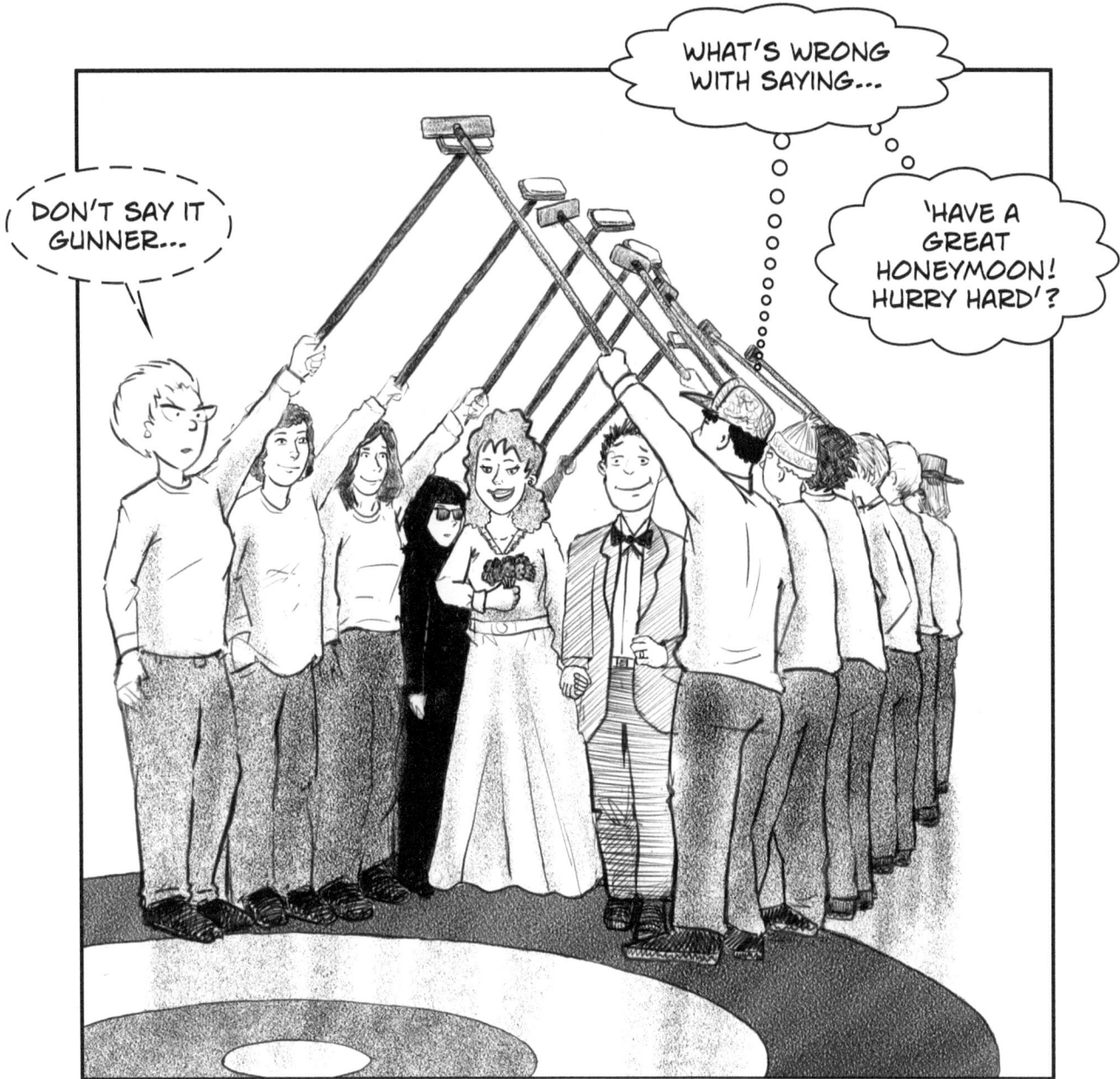

THE GAME FACES OF MALE HOCKEY PLAYERS

THE GAME FACES OF MALE CURLIERS

...IN GRADE SCHOOL...

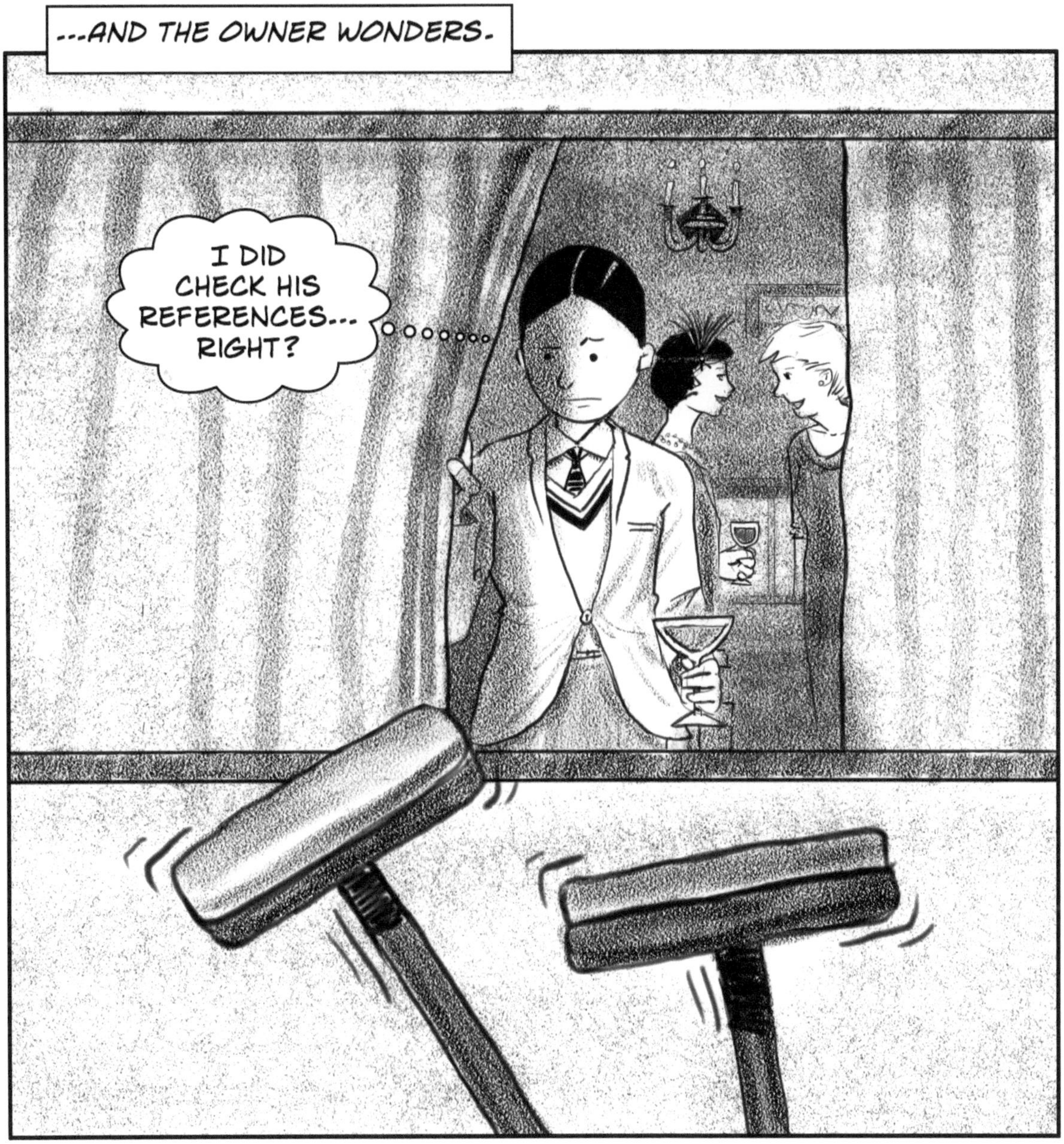
...AND THE OWNER WONDERS.
I DID CHECK HIS REFERENCES... RIGHT?

SHUFFLEBOARD ON ICE? BOCCE BALL?

DUCK HUNTING EXCEPT WITH A BROOM?

SOUTH YUKON REINDEER PICKLE SKATE BALL?

REAL FUNNY ALBERT.

SOME PEOPLE LOVE RIBBING THEIR FRIENDS ABOUT CURLING. EVEN WHILE SPELUNKING. EXPLORING CAVES AND VOIDS DEEP, DEEP UNDERGROUND WHERE SPACES ARE MEASURED IN INCHES. WHERE IT'S SO DARK AND QUIET, ALL YOU CAN SEE IS WHAT YOUR LAMP ILLUMINATES AND ALL YOU CAN HEAR IS YOUR LABORED BREATHING. YOUR HANDS SWEATING TO THE POINT WHERE IT'S HARD TO HOLD A PENCIL OR A PIECE OF CHARCOAL. OR THE CREATIVE MIND IS PARALYZED BY JUST THE **THOUGHT** OF THOUSANDS OF TONS OF ROCK SURROUNDING ME...IN THE DARK.

...ANYWAY...INTRODUCE YOUR FRIENDS TO CURLING. THEY'LL LOVE IT.

ROBOTS TAKE TO THE ICE...

...WITH MIXED RESULTS.
THAT DIDN'T WORK, BUT YOU DIDN'T KILL ANYONE SO THAT'S GOOD.
WHERE ARE YOU GOING? TO PRACTICE I HOPE. YOU STINK.
IN THE LAB, THE PHONE RINGS.
I'M IN THE MIDDLE OF SOMETHING NOW BUT, I'LL TAKE CARE OF IT.
I'M GUESSING ROBOT CURLING ISN'T READY.
PLAN B IS UNDERWAY.

HEY BUDDY, GIVE ME A HAND! MY KNEE IS FROZEN TO THE ICE. I'VE BEEN STUCK HERE FOREVER!
I CAN'T LAST MUCH LONGER!
MY WIFE HAD THE POLICE DECLARE ME MISSING!
WELL, DON'T REST YOUR KNEE ON THE ICE THEN.

THERE IS NO TRASH TALKING OR MIND GAMES IN CURLING.

I WONDER HOW MANY BONES ARE IN THERE!

EVER WONDER HOW THE TONGUE WORKS?

??

BUT IF IT'S YOUR CREEPY LITTLE BROTHER ON THE OTHER TEAM, WELL...

NOLAN!

GET YOUR FINGERS OUT OF YOUR MOUTH AND THROW YOUR ROCK!

ONCE EVERY YEAR, CURLING CLUBS INSTALL NEW ICE FOR THE UPCOMING SEASON. DESPITE THE BEST EFFORTS OF THE ICE MASTERS, AN ODD OCCURRENCE HAPPENS.

BUGS GET FROZEN IN THE ICE.

A BEE AND AN ANT!

OH LOOK, A FLY...

FOUR BEATLES.

FOUR BUGS!

AN ANT AND A HOLE SHAPED LIKE A POSSUM?

U.S. DEPT OF CURLING ICE...

WIGGLE RIVER CURLING HERE...

U.S. DEPT. OF CURLING ICE, WASHINGTON D.C.
BUT, NO ACTUAL OH-POSSUM? JUST AN IMPRESSION IN THE ICE?
NO, JUST BUGS.
JUST COUNT THE BUGS...
THANKS WIGGLE RIVER
34 BUGS AND A HOLE SHAPED LIKE A POSSUM?
YOU HAVE FAILED ME FOR THE LAST TIME, ICE MASTER.
WONDER WHAT HAPPENED TO THE RACCOON...

CURLING ETIQUETTE: ALWAYS BE READY TO PLAY.

THESE ARE NOT FINCHES STEVE.
HONK
HONK
HONK
HONK
HONK
HONK
HONK
HONK
HONK
HONK
HONK
HONK
I BOUGHT THE WRONG BIRD FOOD...
HONK
HONK

YEAH, THAT SEEMS ABOUT RIGHT.

47

48

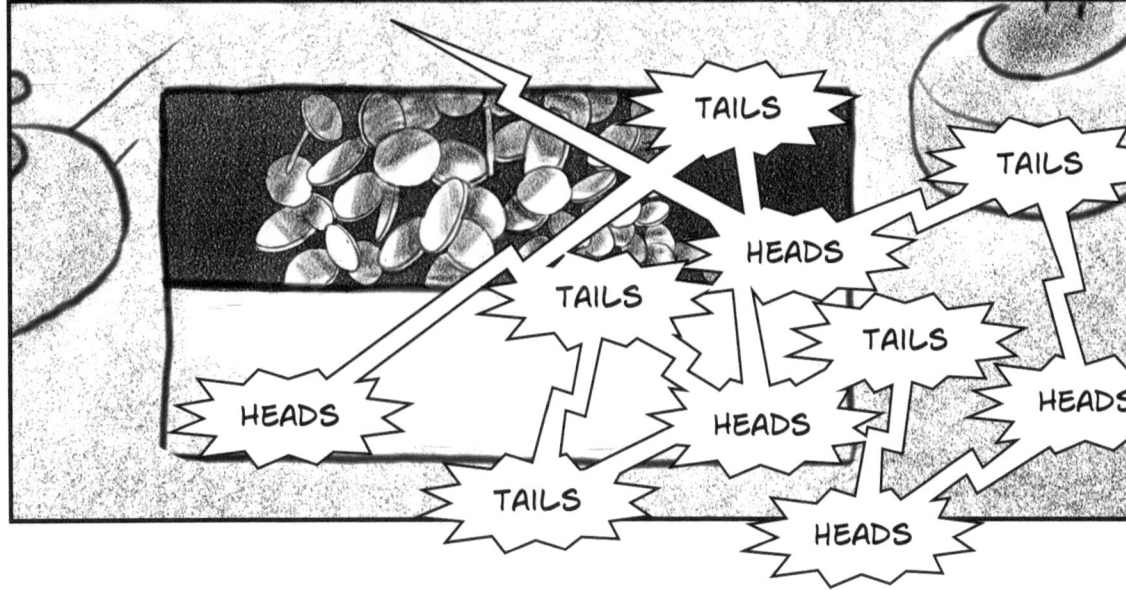

ODDS AND ENDS...

You need to work on your game.

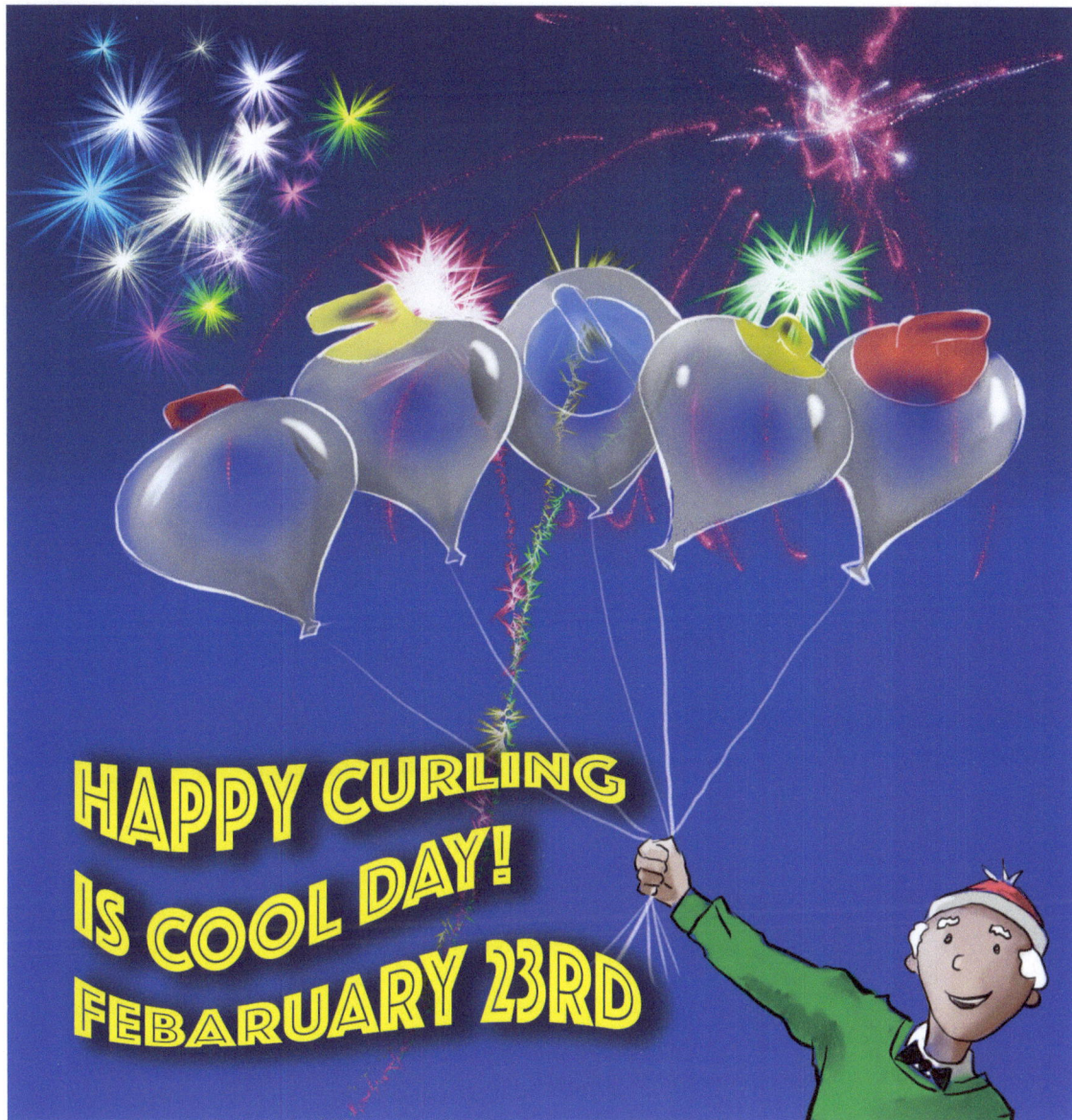

HAPPY CURLING IS COOL DAY!
FEBARUARY 23RD

WHEN ALAN SHEPARD AND EDGAR MITCHELL LANDED ON THE MOON IN 1971 IN APOLLO 14, HISTORY WAS MADE. NOT JUST IN A SCIENTIFIC WAY BUT, IN A SPORTS WAY TOO.

SHEPARD HIT TWO GOLF BALLS USING A MAKESHIFT GOLF CLUB. HE SHANKED THE FIRST BALL BUT HIT THE SECOND FORTY YARDS INTO A CRATER.

VERY COOL BUT, LOW TECH.

AS THE U.S. AGAIN SETS IT'S EYE ON SENDING HUMANS TO THE MOON. NASA IS SAID TO BE EXPLORING NEW SPORTS THAT CAN BE PLAYED IN LOW GRAVITY ENVIRONMENTS...

...CURLING IS SAID TO BE ONE OF THE LEADING CONTENDERS.

A GRITTY CURLING NOVEL THAT'S JUST WAITING TO BE WRITTEN...

Curling Team Art

BEATNIK CURLERS

By Flammy Flunix

$1.25

THEY WERE BORN BAD AND THEY CURL THAT WAY...

SUPERTRAMP MEETS CURLING.

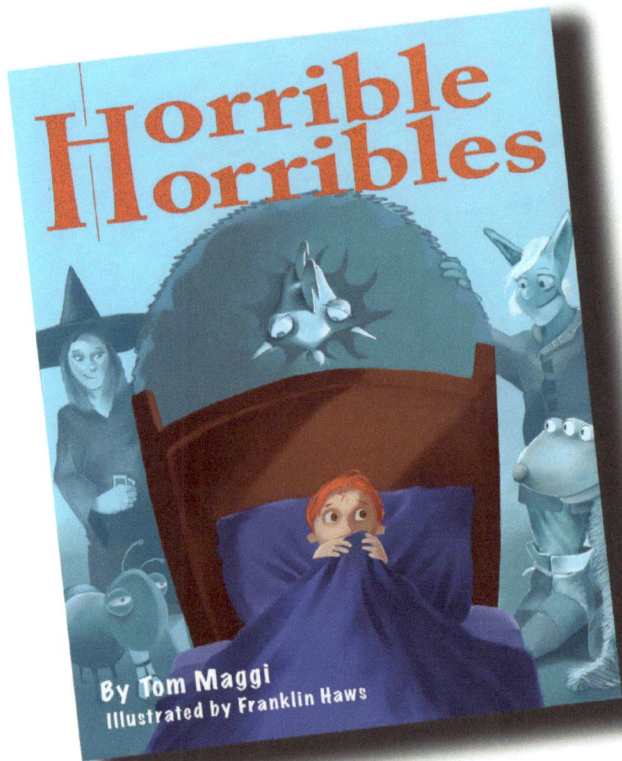

Horrible Horribles

By Tom Maggi
Illustrated by Franklin Haws

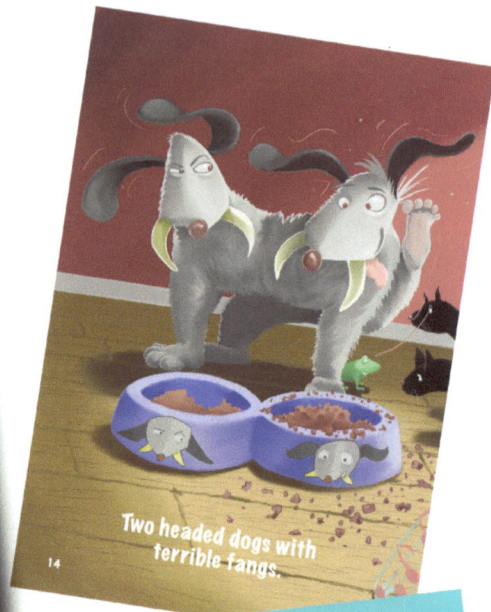

Two headed dogs with terrible fangs.

14

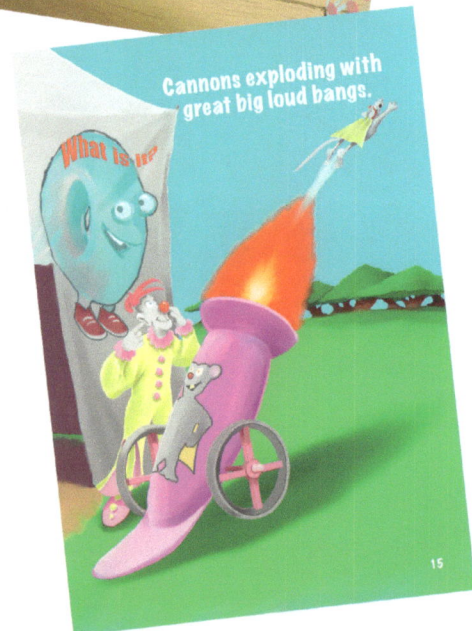

Cannons exploding with great big loud bangs.

What is in

15

AVAILABLE
ON AMAZON!

WRITTEN BY TOM MAGGI
ILLUSTRATED BY
BY FRANKLIN HAWS JR.

Balloon Animals 1
Picture And Coloring Book!
Ages 4-8
Written and Illustrated by Franklin Haws

Balloon Animals 2
Picture and Coloring Book
Ages 4-8
Written and Illustrated by Franklin Haws

Balloon Animals 3
Picture and Coloring Book
Ages 4-8
Written and Illustrated by Franklin Haws

All across Georgia, Leo's sister is known for her interesting taste in furniture. Leo and Trish the goldfish just love his sister's crazy aquarium!

Maureen, Bog the frog, and her collection of stuffed animal are waiting out the rain in Wales. As soon as it stops, they can all go out and play!

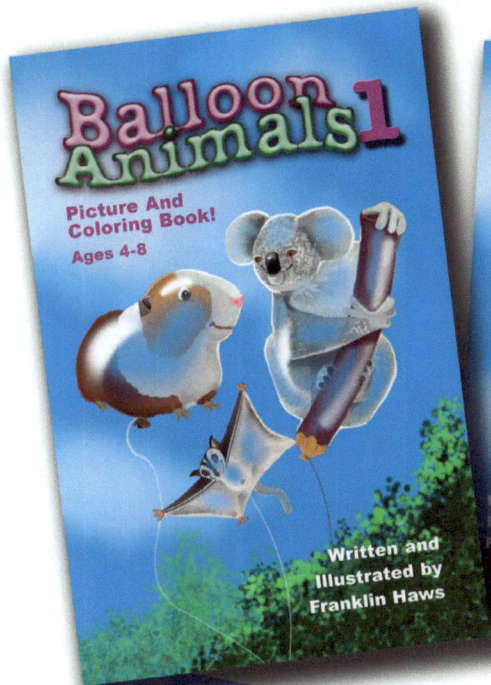

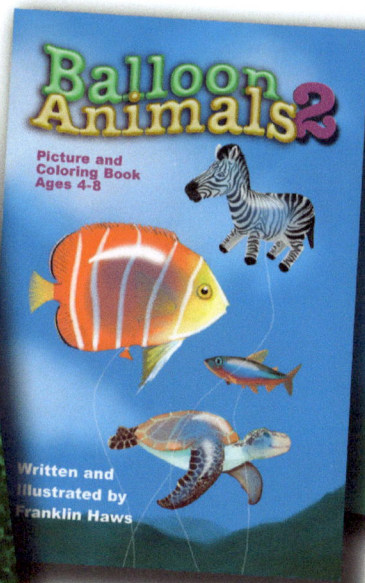

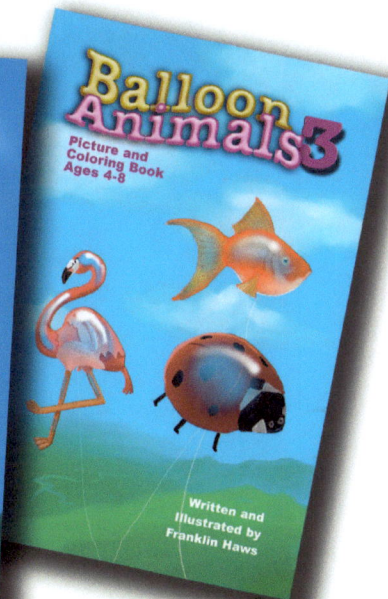

ALL AVAILABLE ON AMAZON!

WRITTEN AND ILLUSTRATED BY FRANKLIN HAWS JR.

Franklin Haws
Digital Illustrator

Franklin Haws is a digital illustrator in the Minneapolis\St. Paul area.

Working exclusively with Corel Painter and Adobe Photoshop, Franklin creates many types colorful illustrations ranging from automotive, aviation, fantasy and children's books.

Humor and vivid colors are evident though out all of Franklin's work.

franklinhaws@hotmail.com

curlingteamart@hotmail.com

franklinhawsartwork.com/

facebook.com/curlingteamart/

facebook.com/Franklins-Artwork

zazzle.com/store/curlingteamart

www.ingramcontent.com/pod-product-compliance
Lightning Source LLC
Chambersburg PA
CBHW041425090426
42741CB00002B/37

* 9 7 8 0 5 7 8 5 9 2 1 9 0 *